# MAGICAL SCIENCE

## MAGIC TRICKS for YOUNG SCIENTISTS

UPDATED

By Eric Ladizinsky

Illustrated by Dianne O'Quinn Burke

LOWELL HOUSE JUVENILE

LOS ANGELES

NTC/Contemporary Publishing Group

*To Lisa, who grows flowers in barren rock —E. L.*

*For Matthew and Djem, with love —D. O. B.*

This edition published 1998 by Lowell House
A division of NTC/Contemporary Publishing Group, Inc.
4255 West Touhy Avenue, Lincolnwood (Chicago), Illinois 60646-1975 U.S.A.
Copyright © 1992, 1998 by NTC/Contemporary Publishing Group, Inc.

Managing Director and Publisher: Jack Artenstein
Director of Publishing Services: Rena Copperman
Editorial Director, Juvenile: Brenda Pope-Ostrow
Director of Juvenile Development: Amy Downing
Director of Art Production: Bret Perry
Update Editor: Joanna Siebert
Designers: Tanya Maiboroda and Lisa Lenthall
Typesetter: Treesha Runnells

Library of Congress Catalog Card Number: 98-66655
ISBN: 1-56565-980-5

Lowell House books can be purchased at special discounts when
ordered in bulk for premiums and special sales.
Contact Customer Service at:
NTC/Contemporary Publishing Group, Inc.
4255 W. Touhy Avenue, Lincolnwood (Chicago), Illinois 60646-1975 U.S.A.
1-800-323-4900

Printed and bound in the United States of America

10 9 8 7 6 5 4 3 2 1

# ★ contents ★

# what's magical about science?

*There's a secret ancient mystics knew,*
*A secret this book reveals to you:*
*The greatest magic show in town*
*Is here and there and all around.*
*In every flower and flying dove*
*In twinkling stars way up above.*
*Nature's magic makes things go—*
*The laws of physics behind the show!*

Since ancient times men and women who have understood the workings of nature have often been considered to possess "magical powers." The ancient astronomers, for instance, knowing a little bit about the orbits of planets, could predict when and where planets would appear in the sky. Their predictions inspired awe in people who were less knowledgeable than they were. The ancient alchemists performed all manner of wondrous feats, simply because they studied and understood the properties of chemicals.

Imagine traveling back in time, perhaps a thousand years ago, taking with you things that are commonplace today—a television, a radio, a laser, a computer. What a powerful wizard you would seem! Imagine what an ancient Egyptian might say if he or she saw a car. "What makes it go?" he or she would ask. "Where are the horses to pull it?"

Perhaps scientists and inventors truly are the greatest magicians of all, for they reveal to us the magic of the universe in which we live. In this book, you'll learn of many natural wonders and the scientific principles that underlie them. You'll learn how to use these simple scientific principles to create some amazing magic tricks.

The tricks are categorized by the particular aspect of the natural world they illuminate (for instance, gravity, mechanics, or chemistry). After learning how each trick works, you'll learn the **science** behind the illusion. To help you learn the language scientists speak, look for the floating boxes of scientific expressions such as the one below. They will help you understand why your magic tricks work.

It's important to understand that being a good magician takes more than just understanding how a trick is done. You must be an entertainer as well. You must help your audience to "suspend their disbelief"—if they are to marvel at the magic of the world.

**Science** is the study and exploration of natural phenomena.

In the following pages, you'll learn how to mesmerize any audience. With a creative costume, a few intriguing tales, and a well-laid show table you can become a master of suspense and illusion as you host your own magical science show. Now, get ready to treat your audience to the magical world of science from the first trick to your final bow.

## A WORD ABOUT SAFETY

**As exciting as science and magic are, they can also be dangerous. Some of the tricks in this book require parental supervision; always observe the guidelines set at the beginning of each experiment and follow the directions exactly.**

# how to host a
# magical science show!

Whether you are showing some friends a few magic tricks or hosting an evening of magic, there are a few essential steps to putting on a show. Adapt each step described in this section to create a unique magical science show that your audience will love—and learn a little science while you're at it!

## Choose the Tricks

The first step to putting on a magical science show is selecting the tricks you want to perform. Flip through this book and choose about five tricks that seem interesting. Try each one to make sure that you like it. Look for tricks that will appeal to your audience. Think about who you will be inviting: Will there be lots of little kids or mostly adults? If there is going to be a mixture of people, then come up with a variety of magic tricks that will appeal to all ages present.

The purpose of having a magic show is to entertain people, so keep this in mind as you prepare. Your show should move along quickly, so when you determine the order, make sure the tricks are easy to set up and follow each other logically. There should not be any lulls or long pauses between tricks that might make your audience feel impatient. You may want to write down several plans before selecting the one that works best. No matter which tricks you choose, always plan an attention-grabbing trick to start off your show. Be sure to end your performance with a really impressive trick that will have them asking about your next show. Once you've decided on your list of tricks, start practicing right away to get ready for the show.

## Set the Stage

Finding the right location is an important part of having a magical science show. If you're having your show at home, choose a room that is spacious, such as a living room or den. If you decide to have it outside, make sure that you have an alternate location in case it's too windy or drizzly. The show table is a crucial element of your location. Set up your table as a stage might be set up, so the attention is focused on your performance. The audience should be seated in front of you. Remember, you don't want the audience to sit too close, where they might be able to see *too much* of the action, but you do want everyone to be able to see you perform.

## Invite the Audience

Make a list of the people you would like to invite to your show. Think about how many people you can seat in the location you have chosen. Choose a time and date that's convenient for your audience. If you're inviting friends your own age, after school may be the best time to have your magical science show. If you're only inviting family members, Saturday afternoon may work best. Depending on the size and extent of your show, you can mail invitations, pass out fliers, or simply spread the word yourself.

You're invited to a ★
Magical Science
Show
hosted by
Rosa "The Great"
★ Johnson
Saturday at 2:00
1126 West Third St.

## Find a Costume

Choose a costume that will have a magical effect on the audience! Think about the type of show you want to put on. Do you want it to be humorous or mysterious? Serious or downright silly? Choose a style that you're comfortable with, but make sure that it will appeal to your audience. Once you decide on the style of the show, putting together a costume will be much easier! Look around your home for any interesting items that can be used as part of your costume. For a magician's costume with a bit of mystery, wear a black flowing robe with a scarf wrapped around your head like a turban. Create a silly look by trying on oversized pants and a brightly colored shirt. To play up the science aspect of your show, wear a lab coat and style your hair until it stands on end. For a traditional appearance, try on a top hat, find a magic wand, and wear an overcoat. If you want to stick with a serious approach, simply dress neatly in your regular clothes.

## Put Together a Prop List

Make a list of the props you will need for each trick, like the one below. Use it as a checklist to gather materials, then double-check the list as you set up your show table. Group the items together on the table by trick so that you can find everything easily. Leave plenty of space in the center of the table to perform, and make sure that none of the props is blocking the audience's view of the action.

| got it? | on the table? | props | trick |
|---------|---------------|-------|-------|
| ✔ | | candle | glassblowing |
| ✔ | | candleholder | glassblowing |
| ✔ | | two glasses of water | glassblowing |
| ✔ | | book | glassblowing |
| ✔ | | matches | glassblowing |

## Practice, Practice, Practice

Being good at magic, like almost any hobby, takes practice. Even a simple trick requires work and patience to get it just right. Find someplace where you can be alone (unless you are doing a trick that requires a parent's supervision). Practice each trick until you can do it without even thinking about the individual movements. Try practicing in front of a mirror to see how a trick will look to an audience. When you think you've got it down, perform the trick in front of a friend. Be sure to choose someone who will not give away your secrets! Ask your friend to watch carefully as you practice each trick and point out anything that you need to improve upon.

## BECOME A STORYTELLER

**Great magicians are also great storytellers. Capture your audience's imagination by telling amazing stories about different times and places. You'll find stories to tell with every trick in this book. Use these or, if you prefer, invent your own. If you use the stories in this book, you may want to change each one so it fits the character you have created for yourself. Learn each story well enough so that it flows easily when you perform a trick. Don't worry about getting the words exactly right. Practice saying the story different ways to find the version that sounds most natural. As long as you can weave an interesting tale about the trick you are performing, the audience will enjoy it. Once you have the story memorized and can do the trick easily, you should start practicing them together.**

### Try It Out

A day or two before the show, conduct a full dress rehearsal. Set up the show table and put on your costume. Ask a friend to watch as you run through the show and point out anything that still needs work. Are you able to avoid uncomfortable breaks in the flow? Are all of your materials easy to find on the table? Do the stories you tell sound natural? Do the tricks come off without a hitch? If you encounter a problem, fix it immediately. You can easily substitute one trick for another or change the order of your show if you need to. Write a few key words or sentences on an index card to use as a prompt if you're having trouble remembering a trick or a story. Also make sure the show isn't too long. It should be about 15 minutes long if there are a lot of kids under eight years old in the audience, or about 30 minutes long for older kids and adults.

## On with the Show!

An hour or so before the show, check that everything is ready. Make sure the seating is arranged the way you want it to be. Set up your show table and double-check your list of props. Get dressed and check your appearance in a mirror. Try to visualize how the show will go in your mind: Picture each trick as you tell the story that goes with it to yourself. When it's time for the show, take a deep breath. Remember, the point of hosting a magic show is to have fun. If a problem arises during a trick, finish it if you can or move on to the next one. You're much more likely to notice a mistake than anyone else.

Be sure to thank the audience for coming when you're through. If the audience demands more when you're finished, go ahead and perform an encore, that is, an additional trick that you have prepared ahead of time. But always keep in mind the two rules of magic, known as a magician's code.

## MAGICIAN'S CODE

**NEVER repeat a trick. Whenever you repeat a trick for the same person or audience, you run the risk of revealing the secret to the magic.**

**NEVER reveal the secrets behind your magic. Magic, once understood, is no longer magical!**

Now you're ready to create some magical science!

# ★ genie's fists ★

*Have you ever wanted to be Hercules*
*And move giant things as you please?*
*With just the strength of a feather*
*And by being really clever,*
*You can move the unmovable with ease.*

## MAGIC

## You Will Need

• assistant

## Getting Ready

For this trick, you'll need a large assistant (perhaps an older brother or sister or a parent) to play the part of a giant stone Genie. He or she will need to memorize a few lines before performance time. Have your assistant stand at your side during the trick.

## Performing the Trick

**1** Now take your audience to another time and place by telling them a story. Tell them, "I once sailed with a gallant crew across the seven seas. During one violent storm my mates and I were shipwrecked on a mysterious island in the Indian Ocean. When we awoke from the crash, we found ourselves in a magnificent golden palace, the door of which was guarded by a giant statue of stone."

**2** Have your assistant face the audience, extend his or her arms, put one fist on top of the other, and close his or her eyes. Then say, "The statue was of a mighty sleeping Genie who stood with his fists stacked one on top of the other." Then say, "Suddenly the stone Genie opened its eyes and began to speak!"

**3** Your assistant, playing the part of the Genie, should then say loudly, "Unless you can break the bonds of my stone fists, you will be prisoners here forever!"

**4** Now say, "The Genie had spoken. We would have to separate the giant stone fists to ever leave that place! Can any of you break the bonds of the fists?" Ask a volunteer to come up. As your assistant presses his or her fists together with all his or her strength, ask the volunteer to try to pull the fists apart in the vertical direction. He or she will find it difficult or impossible to do so.

**5** Then say, "The strongest members of our crew also could not pull or pound the Genie's fists apart. But in watching my mates' helpless struggle, I found the answer."

**6** Have your assistant press his or her fists tightly together again. (Make sure his or her arms are fully extended.) Then slap two fingers of either hand against each of the two fists as shown, separating the fists, not crossing them.

**7** Then your assistant should say, "You have learned a great secret—the softest of blows can defeat the mightiest of foes. The golden doors are now open and you are free to leave. Farewell, magician!"

## SCIENCE

Why was it so easy to separate the fists? One way to understand why is to think about moving a friend on ice skates. It's a lot easier to push your friend forward than to lift her or him up into the air. Why? Because when you try to lift your friend up vertically, you have to fight a large force—the force of the earth's **gravity** pulling down on your friend.

> **Gravity** is an invisible force field that all objects produce. Each object's force field attracts other objects around it. Small objects have very weak fields, but massive objects (like the earth) have very large fields.

When you push your friend forward horizontally, you don't have to fight gravity. The only force you have to fight is the friction of the blades against the ice, which is much weaker than the gravitational force and is easier to overcome.

When your assistant pressed his or her fists together, he or she pushed the top fist down and pulled the bottom fist up. All the force generated was in the up/down, or vertical, direction. So when your volunteer tried to pull your assistant's fists apart in that direction, he or she had to fight all this force. Since the assistant didn't push his or her fists together horizontally, very little force was generated in that direction, making it easy to knock the fists apart sideways.

# electrical storm

Electricity

*From the lightning in storms*
*To the beeping of horns,*
*To a toaster's glow that warms*

*In every gadget that blinks*
*And every magnet that clinks,*
*It's charges behind these high jinks.*

**MAGIC**

## You Will Need

- silk cloth
- tissue paper
- bowl
- drinking glass

- wooden or plastic table
  (if the table you have available is
  metal, cover it with a tablecloth)

## Getting Ready

**1** Make sure the silk cloth is dry.

**2** Tear the tissue paper into very small
pieces and put them in the bowl.

**3** Wash and dry your hands thoroughly.
(It's important that your hands be
completely dry before performing this trick.)

**4** Put the silk cloth, the bowl of tissue paper, and the
glass (upside down) on your show table.

## Performing the Trick

**1** Begin this trick by telling your audience: "On one of my travels into the remote mountains of the Himalayas, I discovered a remarkable tribe of people. They lived in one of the coldest places on the earth, but all they had to wear was strange silk clothing that couldn't possibly protect them from the freezing storms."

**2** Pick up the silk from the table and hold it in front of you. Then say, "This is a piece of that special cloth. The members of the tribe told me it was made from magical silk spun by an enchanted worm—named Barney."

**3** Use the silk to set the glass right side up on the table, then rub it inside and outside with the silk cloth. While rubbing, say, "They also told me that anything rubbed with the magical silk would be protected from the mightiest storms and the freezing cold."

**4** Continue to rub the glass for two minutes or more. Now use the silk to set the glass upside down on the table as shown, without your hand touching the glass.

**5** Pick up the bowl of tissue pieces and take a pinch of them in one hand. Hold them 8" to 10" above the glass. Then say, "And now, by rubbing this glass I have made it magical, too! Any snow that touches the glass will be cast off."

**6** Sprinkle the tissue paper "snow" onto the glass and watch the magic. The tissue pieces will first stick to the glass and then fly off in an amazing way!

 SCIENCE ★

Wow! What's going on? What strange invisible force is responsible for the tissue's sticking to the glass and then flying off it?

Well, not only flying tissue but also nearly everything else you experience—from lightning to starlight to television—results from something called **charge**.

We know of two different types of charges, positive and negative. If two charged particles have the same charge (such as two negative charges), they will repel, or push away from, each other. Oppositely charged particles will attract each other, or come together. Most of the things around you—such as tables, trees, and air—contain about an equal number of negative and positive charges. Thus, the charges cancel each other out. That's why most of the time you don't notice their effect.

When you rubbed the glass with the silk, however, the glass "stole" (stripped off) negatively charged particles from the silk. The glass had more negative charges than positive, so it became negatively charged.

When you dropped the paper bits, the extra negative charges on the glass attracted the positive charges in the tissue bits (remember that opposite charges attract). This caused the paper to stick to the glass. Once the paper and glass touched, however, some of the extra negative charges on the glass leaked onto the paper. Can you guess why? They were trying to get away from each other (remember that like charges repel each other), so the paper bits very quickly became negatively charged, too. Since the glass and the bits were both negatively charged, the paper bits flew off!

> **Charge** is a quality that some microscopic particles have. Charged particles create invisible force fields around them that can affect (attract or repel) other charged particles.

# grate vision

Have you ever seen a solid fence "disappear"?
Bet you have!

*If you've ever ridden in a car or on a bike*
*And happened to speed by a fence or the like,*
*Then just like Superman using X-ray vision,*
*The fence disappeared out of sight.*

MAGIC

## You Will Need

- tracing paper, 8½" x 11"
- smooth, flat surface
- ruling pen (this is a special kind of pen used for drawing thin lines)

- ruler
- book or newspaper with medium to large print

## Getting Ready

**1** For this trick, you'll need to make a magic grating. Begin by laying the tracing paper down on a flat, smooth surface.

**2** Now, using the pen and ruler, draw side-by-side (parallel) lines about ⅛" apart all the way across the tracing paper.

**3** Make a crisscross pattern by drawing more parallel lines ⅛" apart at a 90° angle to the lines already drawn.

**4** Starting from the upper left corner and working toward the lower right corner, draw more parallel lines, this time on the diagonal of the paper. Don't forget to keep the lines ⅛" apart.

**5** Finish your magic grating by drawing one last set of diagonal parallel lines from the upper right corner of the tracing paper down to the lower left corner.

## Performing the Trick

**1** Ask the members of your audience to gather around your show table.

**2** Place your book or newspaper on the table and ask one volunteer to turn to any page.

**3** With your magic grating, cover the page selected.

**4** Ask your volunteers to try to read through the grating. They will find it impossible.

**5** Now say, "It is often said that a magician's hand is quicker than the eye. I have learned to move so fast that I can remove the grating, read what is underneath, and replace the grating—all in the blink of an eye."

**6** Slightly wet the fingertips of your right hand by licking them, then lean over the book and put your fingers over the lower right corner of the grating (if you're left-handed, put your fingers over the lower left corner). Tell your volunteers: "You may see a little shaking of the paper between your blinking, but you won't see me remove it. Catch me if you can!"

**7** Now shake the grating back and forth over the page, using small rapid movements (you only have to shake the grating about ¼" to ½"). You will be able to see through the grating and read what's underneath. Amaze your audience by reading the covered page out loud.

## SC ENCE

Why can you see through the grating when you shake it, but not when it's still? Why does the grating seem to disappear? Why does a fence seem to disappear as you speed by it on a bicycle? The answer lies in many of the familiar objects around you.

Our eyes send messages to the brain that tell us what image we are seeing. The brain holds on to those messages for a short time. So even after an image is gone, your brain still sees it momentarily.

When something moves very fast, as does the grating in your trick, your brain does not have enough time to "see" it clearly. So your brain does something very interesting: It ignores what it can't see very well, especially if there is something easier to see lying in the same direction.

## How is your grating like an electric fan?

A good way to understand what's going on in your trick is to use an analogy. That means using an idea you already understand in order to understand another idea. Consider an electric fan—it's very similar to your grating. When the fan is off, the wide blades block most of your view of the other side. Turn the fan on and the blades seem to melt away—you can see right through the spinning fan as if the blades weren't there. In fact, you can see entire objects sitting behind the fan, even though you know that only a tiny portion of the objects can be seen between the blades at any given time. Why is that?

As the blades rotate, the spaces between them also rotate. These rotating spaces allow you to see all the different parts of the objects behind the fan. Your brain then stores, or remembers, all the parts and puts them together to form complete pictures. Meanwhile, it ignores what it can't see very well—the spinning blades—so all you see are the objects.

Your grating works the same way as the blades of a fan. When the grating is moved quickly, the tiny spaces between the lines reveal small bits of the page underneath. Your brain collects the bits of information, allowing you to construct a picture of the book underneath—which you can read!

# fire trail

**Parental Supervision Required**

Have you ever heard of a combustion engine?

*An engine makes every car go—*
*How it works is a thing you should know.*
*A neat trick with matches*
*Makes invisible gases*
*The secret behind the show!*

## You Will Need

- two wooden matches (wax coated)
- matchbox
- glass of water

## Getting Ready

Put the matches, matchbox, and glass of water on your show table.

## Performing the Trick

**1** Look at your audience and say, "One of the hazards of travel-ing back into the past is that I often end up in time periods before any modern conveniences were around—no electricity or hot water, no air-conditioning or refrigerators. Try finding your way to the bathroom in the middle of the night in a dark medieval castle!"

**2** Now pick up the two matches and say, "So I developed a way to make a flame jump. Without leaving my bedside, I'd light one match and make the tiny flame jump from one candle to the next to light my way before getting out of bed."

**3** Light the two matches and hold one match over the other match as shown. Now say, "Watch closely to see the flame jump."

2" to 3"

**4** Blow out the bottom match. Make sure the rising smoke from the bottom match flows up into the match flame above it. The bottom match will magically light!

smoke trail

**5** Blow out the bottom match two or three more times and let it relight as before. Just before you relight it, say, "Flame, jump!" Put both matches into the glass of water.

# SCIENCE

Do you know why the match caught fire without being touched? Since it only happens when the smoke from one match flows into the flame of the other, the smoke must carry something with it. What does it carry?

When matches burn, chemicals in the wood and air react to produce heat and light. The matches also release chemicals in the form of gas into the air around them. In your trick, this gas flowed up into the flame above when you blew out the bottom match. The gas became hot—so hot that it exploded—sending more heat down the smoke trail. That heat relit the bottom match.

## Gasoline, sparks, and energy

When gasoline and air mix together, they also form a gas that explodes when heated (in this case by a spark). The energy from the explosion makes cars go.

So why are car engines called combustion engines?

It is interesting to note that your trick would not have worked with just any kind of matches. Not every burning object releases an explosive gas around it. It depends on what the object is made of. Gases that explode or burn when heated are combustible. That's why car engines are called combustion engines. And, you could say you performed a combustible trick!

# ★ change of mind

As time goes on, people learn more and more about the brain and all the amazing things it can do. People just like you have invented complicated machines such as computers and spaceships. Who knows what amazing things we will be able to do with our brains a hundred years from now? The possibilities are endless. With a little trickery and careful scientific observation, you can appear to have advanced mental powers right now. You can even appear to read minds!

MAGIC

## You Will Need

- blindfold
- coin
- two chairs

## Getting Ready

Place the blindfold and the coin on your show table, and put the chairs side by side next to the table.

## Performing the Trick

**1** Begin your trick by telling your audience: "Not long ago, I took a trip through time—into the future. I found that the people of the future spend a lot of time developing their mental powers. They have even learned how to read the thoughts of others. I became good friends with these people, and they taught me their secrets. Now I, too, have mastered their mind-reading techniques." Then look at your audience, open your eyes really wide, raise your arms, and say, "I will now give you a glimpse of the future."

**2** Ask two volunteers to come up and sit in the two chairs.

**3** Give the coin to one of the volunteers.

**4** Now tie the blindfold around your head, making sure to cover your eyes completely. Turn your back to the volunteers.

**5** Tell your volunteers: "The two of you must now secretly decide who shall hide the coin. Then, whoever has it must hold it in one hand."

**6** When the volunteers have decided, the magic begins. Ask both volunteers to close their hands into fists.

**7** With your back still to your volunteers, tell them: "Please hang your fists down by your sides, both of you. Now, whoever has the coin, raise the coin to your forehead. Remember, don't tell me who has the coin."

**8** Now tell your subjects: "I want the person with the coin to concentrate really hard. Think of nothing else but the coin. The other volunteer must empty his or her mind and let his or her thoughts wander."

**9** While your volunteers are concentrating, tell the audience: "The mental energy of the person with the coin is slowly seeping into the coin. This 'brain energy' is strongest near the head. I will be able to see this invisible 'brain energy' because of my advanced mental powers."

**10** Tell both volunteers to put their fists on their knees, knuckles up.

**11** Quickly remove your blindfold, turn around, and look at the backs of your volunteers' hands. Pretend to be thinking really hard. One person's hands will look the same. The other person's hands will look a little different from each other. One hand will seem darker than the other, and its veins will look larger and puffier. This was the hand hanging to the side. The lighter-colored hand, the one with smaller veins, is the one that held the coin to the volunteer's forehead.

**12** Touch the lighter hand of the volunteer whose hands look different and say, "Ah, the coin is here and so are your thoughts!"

**hand held down is darker in color**

**hand held up is lighter in color**

SCIENCE

What's going on? Did "brain energy" really change the color of your volunteer's hands?

Well, it's not really brain energy. In fact, it's just our old friend gravity. Remember Genie's Fists (page 11)? The earth's gravity pulls everything down, including the blood in your body. The only thing that can get blood to flow up against gravity is your heart. Your heart acts as a little pump pushing blood to all parts of the body, but it's harder for your heart to push blood up, fighting gravity, than down.

The hand that the volunteer held to his or her forehead was above the heart. That hand had less blood flowing to it than the hand hanging below the heart. The hanging hand was thus darker than the hand held to the forehead. The veins were also more swollen.

# on pins and needles

**Parental Supervision Required**

Why do you need something sharp to cut something tough apart? Why can a pin puncture your skin? If you could see things microscopic, you'd have a handle on this topic. With sharp edges and sharp tips, it's smallness that does the trick!

MAGIC

## You Will Need

- sharp needle (not too thin)
- cork
- goggles
- metal file
- 3" nail

- two books of the same thickness
- quarter
- hammer

## Getting Ready

**1** Put the needle into the cork so that the sharp tip sticks out about an inch from the bottom of the cork.

**2** While wearing the goggles to protect your eyes, file the sharp end of the nail until it is almost flat.

filed-down nail

28

**3** Put the two books, the quarter, the needle and cork, the nail, and the hammer on your show table.

## Performing the Trick

**1** Place the two books on the table side by side, leaving about a half-inch space between them. Place the quarter over the space as shown.

½"

**2** Now look at the audience and say, "It may be hard to believe, but at one time steel, glass, and plastic didn't exist. People eventually made these things by mixing together all sorts of chemicals and minerals found in the air and ground. People are always trying to make things stronger and lighter by playing with different materials."

**3** Pick up the cork with the needle in it and show it to the audience. Say, "When I was in the future, the people of the future gave me this needle. It is made of advanced materials and is stronger than our strongest steel, and I'll prove it to you."

**4** Ask a volunteer to come up. Say, "I want you to take this modern, but primitive, nail and try to tap it gently through this quarter by using the hammer." Nothing will happen.

**5** Center the coin between the books again and place the needle tip at the center of the coin.

½"

**6** Say, "Now watch what happens when I use this little needle!" Strike the top of the cork with the hammer (not too hard). The needle will go right through the coin!

**7** Now exclaim: "Wow! And this needle is many times smaller than the nail. Imagine what amazing things we could build with this kind of material!"

 SCIENCE

In reality, the nail and the needle are both made of steel. So why does one penetrate the coin while the other doesn't?

You can understand this trick by referring to Friendly Float (page 41). If all the weight had been carried by one person, it would have been impossible to lift the floater. But when all of your friends lifted the floater together, the weight was distributed evenly. Each lifted only a small part of the weight, making it easier to lift the floater.

The coin is made up of incredibly small particles called atoms. The atoms are stuck together by **chemical bonds**. These bonds can withstand only a certain amount of force before they break. When you placed the needle against the coin, it came in contact with relatively few bonds. That's because the needle is very small at its sharp tip. When the needle was hit with the hammer, the bonds in the coin that came in contact with the needle were subjected to enough force to break them, allowing the needle to go through the coin.

The tip of the nail was much larger, however, especially after the top was filed flat. It came in contact with a lot more bonds. This time, the force of the hammer blow was shared between a lot more bonds. Each bond thus received a much smaller portion of the force. The smaller force on each bond was not enough to break them, so the nail couldn't go through the coin. Something similar happened in Friendly Float. In holding up a floater, each person can withstand only so much weight before he or she "breaks," like a bond, and the floater falls from his or her grip. When more people share the weight—that is, when there are more "bonds"—they can carry the weight between them. Their bonds withstand the force and don't break.

> **A chemical bond** forms when charged particles in different atoms interact, causing the atoms to stick together. Each place where an atom sticks to another is called a bond.

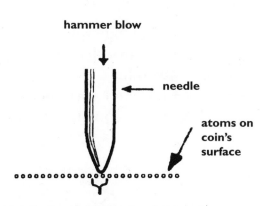

the needle tip contacts only a few bonds

the hammer tip contacts many more bonds

# ★ balancing wand ★

Do you think it would be hard to walk a tightrope in space? Actually, it would be easy because there's nothing pulling you down in space. There's no gravity there. That's why astronauts float. Here on Earth, gravity is constantly pulling you and everything else down. And unless you have good balance, even walking isn't so easy. Remember when you couldn't walk? By making a magic wand just right, you can learn what it takes to walk upright.

MAGIC

## You Will Need

- scissors
- black construction paper
- ruler
- wooden dowel (approximately 10" long and ⅞" thick)
- glue
- masking tape
- two 1-oz. lead fishing weights
- hammer (optional)
- white construction paper

## Getting Ready

**1** Cut a strip of black paper 10" long and 2" wide.

**2** Roll the paper strip tightly around the dowel as shown. Glue down the overlapping edge so the paper forms a tube. Until the glue dries, the tube can be held closed with a strip of masking tape.

**3** When the glue is dry, remove the masking tape and slide the dowel out from the paper tube.

**4** Now put the fishing weights into the tube. (If they are too large, pound them flat with a hammer.)

**5** Cut two 2" x 2" pieces of white construction paper for the wand's tips. Neatly close and glue the ends of the black paper tube as shown.

## Performing the Trick

**1** Gaze into your audience and ask: "Have any of you ever been to the planet Graviton? Well, you'd remember if you had. When I was there, all I did was fall down a lot. Graviton is circled by a moon called Nemesis, just as the earth is orbited by our moon. But Nemesis isn't small like our moon. It's huge. As it goes around Graviton, the direction of gravity keeps changing. It pulls down, then up, then sideways. Living on Graviton is a constant balancing act."

**2** Pick up the wand and hold it out. Then say, "This wand is from Graviton. It has remarkable properties to deal with the constantly changing gravity."

**3** Now balance the wand on your finger as shown. (Make sure the weights are in the middle of your wand, or this won't work!)

**4** Say to the audience, "Now imagine Nemesis circling around above us to the east." Hold the wand and slowly make a circle in the air to imitate Nemesis circling around. As you circle the wand, let the weights fall down to one end.

**5** Ask a member of your audience to try to balance the wand the way you did. Your volunteer won't be able to do it.

**6** Then say, "The wand from Graviton has changed its balance point." Lay the weighted end of the wand on the edge of a table as shown. The weights will keep your balancing wand from falling over the edge.

**7** Now pick up the wand and balance it on the tip of your finger!

# SCIENCE

Do you know why you could balance the wand on your finger? And why the wand did not fall over the edge of the table? Let's find out.

Try to balance a ruler on your finger. After a couple of tries, you'll discover that the ruler balances most easily when you hold your finger in the middle of it. That's the point where the ruler weighs the same amount on either side of your finger. This middle point is called the center of gravity. An object can be balanced at its center of gravity because the weight of the object has been equally distributed.

But what if one end of the ruler is heavier than the other end? In other words, what if its weight is not equally distributed? Because gravity works by pulling an object down at its heaviest point, the ruler would now balance at the heavier end. This time the center of gravity is at that heavier end. If you had used a normal wand in your magic trick, you would not have been able to change its center of gravity. But by adding the fishing weights to the wand and moving them around, you could change it. The volunteer from your audience could not balance the wand on his or her finger as you did because you had changed the center of gravity—from the center of the wand to one end of it. With the wand's center of gravity now at one of its ends, you could balance it on the edge of the table!

34

# glassblowing

**Parental Supervision Required**

*The pushing of air to and fro*
*Causes vacuums that make the winds blow.*
*From a push on a bike racer's ride,*
*To great storms from which you would hide,*
*The filling of vacuums with air*
*Helps racers or makes storms that scare.*

MAGIC

## You Will Need

- two glasses of water
- candle with candleholder
- book
- matches

## Getting Ready

**1** Set up one glass of water and the candle as shown. Make sure the wick is aligned with the center of the glass. If either the glass or the candle is too short, use a book to align their heights.

candle flame at center of glass

**2** Now light the candle. Blow out the match, then drop it into the other glass of water.

**3** Get on the side of the glass opposite the candle and blow at the middle of the first glass. You might blow the candle out. It is more likely you will need to move closer to the glass or farther away from it while blowing at the middle of it in order to find the perfect distance for blowing out the candle.

**4** When you find the exact distance, remember it for your trick.

## Performing the Trick

**1** Set up the first glass of water and candle exactly as you did before.

**2** Look at the audience and say, "I once went to Venice, Italy, to learn the delicate art of glassblowing. I wandered through the streets looking for a teacher."

**3** Now light the candle, drop the match into the second glass of water, and say, "I found a small shop that had 'GLASSBLOWING' written above the door. Inside I met a strange old woman who told me that she did not teach how to blow beautiful shapes out of glass, but taught instead the ancient magic of blowing *through* solid glass."

**4** Get on the opposite side of the glass from the candle, just as you practiced before, and blow the candle out.

# SCIENCE

How did the air you blew get through the glass and blow out the candle? Can you guess?

The trick is that the air blown on your side of the glass caused air to be sucked toward the side of the glass next to the candle. How did that happen? Look at the picture below.

**Molecules** are the smallest particles of every substance including air, water, glass, and stone.

When you blew on the glass, air **molecules** collided with the glass and were deflected outward as shown. As the deflected molecules moved away from the glass, they collided with and swept away other air molecules surrounding the glass. That left an area in back of the glass with fewer molecules. The air in back of the glass thus had a lower **density** of air.

Because the air in back of the glass had a lower density than the area in front of the glass, a small **vacuum** was created. Air around the glass then rushed into this area to replace the molecules that had been swept away. The rush of air blew out the candle.

A moving object, such as a car, will push air aside in the same way and cause air to rush in behind it. Race-car drivers, bicyclists, and long-distance runners will often get behind another racer to take advantage of the in-rushing air, which gives them a push and saves their energy. This strategy is called drafting.

**Density** is the amount of stuff, such as molecules, in a certain volume of space. A **vacuum** is a region of space that has a very low density of gas.

flame

incoming air — glass

air rushes in to fill gap

air molecules blown out of place

*Why do some things float while other things sink?*
*Hmm, what do you think?*
*With some eggs and salt and $H_2O$,*
*You'll find the answer in your magic show!*

**Fluid Statics**

## You Will Need

- three tall drinking glasses
- pitcher of water
- large bowl
- large container of salt

- long-handled spoon
- three eggs
- pen

**first pour salt water into glass**

**then very slowly pour in the pure water**

## Getting Ready

**1** Pour three glasses of water into the large bowl.

**2** Add salt to the water and mix. Keep adding salt until an egg will float in the bowl.

**3** Fill one glass with pure water. Fill the second glass with salt water from the bowl. Fill the third glass halfway with salt water, then very slowly pour pure water on top of the salt water so that it flows gently along the side of the glass. If you pour slowly enough, the pure water will not mix with the salt water.

**4** Place the three glasses on your show table. Be careful not to shake them up! Empty the large bowl, then put it on the table with the three eggs, pen, and spoon.

**5** It is important that you know which glass is which. For your trick, you'll need to remember that an egg will sink in the glass of pure water, float on top of the salt water, and float in the middle of the half-and-half glass.

## Performing the Trick

**1** Ask two volunteers to come up to your show table to assist you.

**2** Have one of the volunteers use the pen to write different labels on the eggs. Have him or her write *sink* on one egg, *float* on another, and *hover* on the third.

**3** Now take the egg marked *sink* and say, "OK, now everybody concentrate. Think *sink*!" Gently drop the egg into the glass filled with pure water. The egg will sink to the bottom.

**4** Now take the egg marked *float* and say, "Concentrate again, please. Everybody think *float*!" Drop the egg into the glass of salt water. It will float!

**5** Finally, take the egg marked *hover* and tell your two volunteers: "I want one of you to think *sink* and the other to think *float*. Let's see who has the more powerful magic." Gently drop the egg into the glass filled with salt water and pure water. The egg will float in the middle of the glass. Look at them and say, "You are equally powerful!"

**6** Pour the eggs and water into the bowl and challenge anyone else to repeat the trick.

# SCIENCE

Do you know why the eggs floated in salt water but sank in pure water? What's different about pure water and salt water? By carefully observing what happens when you make the salt water, you'll get a clue that will unravel the secret.

When you add salt to the water and mix it, it seems to disappear, but the level of the water in the bowl doesn't change (it doesn't rise or sink). You actually fit more stuff in the same amount of space. Whereas just the water filled the space before, now the salt and the water fill the space. Thus, the salt water contains more stuff, or molecules, in a certain **volume** than does regular water. A certain volume of salt water, therefore, weighs more than an equal volume of pure water.

> The **volume** of an object is the amount of space it takes up, or occupies.

When you drop an egg in a glass of water (salty or pure), it can't dissolve the way salt can. It has to make room for itself, so it pushes a volume of water that's equal to its own size out of the way. The sides of the glass don't allow the egg to push water sideways, so the only way it can push the water is up, against gravity. The water also has weight and pushes back.

If the egg weighs more than the volume of water it needs to displace, it sinks and the water level rises. If the water is heavier than the egg, the egg won't be able to push the water up. The egg then floats. From the results of your magic trick, you can see that the egg is heavier than pure water but lighter than salt water.

Why did the egg labeled *hover* float in the middle of the glass?

# friendly float

One of the most amazing powers humans have is the ability to cooperate with one another. By working together, we can do things that seem impossible. The building of the great pyramids of Egypt and our rocket trips to the moon may seem like magic, but they are simply the result of many people sharing their ideas and working together.

By cooperating with some friends, you can make someone appear to float in the air by just touching him or her with your fingertips!

MAGIC

## You Will Need

• four good friends

## Getting Ready

**1** Find a place with plenty of room, such as your basement, living room, or den. You can even perform this trick outside on the grass.

**2** To become good at this trick, you'll need to practice it with your friends a few times before performing it in front of an audience.

## Performing the Trick

**1** Gather your four friends together and choose the smallest one to be the "floater."

**2** Tell the floater to stand very straight and stiff like a robot. If he or she is too relaxed, it will be hard to make the trick work.

**3** Now instruct your friends to move into the positions shown here and below. One person should stand behind the floater and put his or her index fingers under the floater's arms. Two other friends should squat down and each put one index finger under the floater's heels. The magician stands in front of the floater with one finger under the floater's chin.

**4** When everyone is ready, tell your audience: "Friendship is one of the most magical things in the world. With our Friendship Power, we will raise the spirits and the body of our friend. Our friend will float on an invisible sea of our good feelings. Now, everybody think good thoughts about our friend."

**5** Now tell your friends to lift together by counting, "One, two, three, lift!" It is important that the floater remain stiff and all four friends raise their fingers up together. Raise the floater as high as you can, then gently lower him or her back to the ground.

# SCIENCE

What's the secret behind the floating mystery? The best way to understand it is to try the following experiment. Take a small salad plate and try to balance it on one finger. Be careful not to drop and break it! It will balance when your finger is in the middle of the plate—that is, at its center of gravity. There is an equal amount of weight on either side of the center of gravity.

If you want to share the weight of the plate equally with someone else, both of you must hold it the same distance away from its center of gravity and on opposite sides of it. If four people want to share the weight equally, they must surround the plate's center of gravity. You can see this for yourself by asking three friends to help you hold up the plate as shown. Notice that by surrounding the center of gravity, you are sharing the plate's weight equally. If one person were to move his finger closer to the middle of the plate, that person would support less weight, and it would be harder for the other three to hold up the plate. This is what happened in your magic trick.

Your floater's center of gravity is approximately in the middle of his or her body. The lifting points were chosen carefully; they surrounded the floater's center of gravity so all four people could share the weight equally. With each of you having only one-quarter of the floater's weight to lift, you could use only your fingertips to make your friend float in the air!

# ★ the rising tide ★

**Parental Supervision Required**

Have you ever wondered where great storms come from? Where do they get the power to lift millions of gallons of water miles into the sky—water that eventually falls to the earth as gentle rain? In a very small way, you can create the same invisible force that powers storms, re-creating the magic of nature.

MAGIC

## You Will Need

- knife
- cork
- four wooden matches
- dinner plate

- tall, thin drinking glass (wide enough to fit over the cork)
- pitcher of water

## Getting Ready

**1** Cut the cork in half lengthwise, from the top of the cork to the bottom. Ask your mom or dad to help you do this.

**2** Stick three wooden matches into the cork as shown, making your own little Viking ship.

**3** Place the Viking ship, the dinner plate, the drinking glass, the pitcher of water, and the fourth match on your show table.

## Performing the Trick

**1** Now it's time to tell the audience a story. Say, "It is often said that long before Columbus discovered America, ancient Viking ships landed there. But the Vikings did not have the giant wooden sailing ships that Columbus had. They had only tiny ships to sail the dangerous waters. How could they have survived the long, treacherous storms of the wild seas?" Pause dramatically, then say, "Now it's time to tell the tale."

**2** Pick up the pitcher of water and say, "In here I have the water of the oceans." Pour the water onto the dinner plate until the water is about ¼" deep in the middle of the plate.

**3** Show your audience the cork with the matches in it. Tell them: "This cork is made from the wood of an ancient Viking ship. This magical wood can do amazing things."

**4** Place the cork on the water and say, "Imagine this is a tiny Viking ship at sea. When the sailors saw a storm approaching, they would light the torches and go below deck." Light the matches on the cork and drop the match you used to light them in the pitcher of water.

**5** Pick up the glass and say, "When the storm got really bad, the torches were blown out. Then the magic wooden ship cast a spell on the water."

**6** Slowly lower the glass over the little Viking ship until it hits the bottom of the plate. Gently hold the glass down until the matches go out and the water under the cork rises. Once the water rises as high as it will go, gently let go of the glass. The water will stay high in the glass!

**7** Then say, "This is the secret of the Viking sailors: When the torches went out, the magic wood drew up a giant column of water. This allowed the boat to sail safely above the greatest waves and survive the storm!"

 SCIENCE ★

What's happening? How could the water rise when gravity is constantly pulling it down? Is this really magical wood?

You can begin to understand what's going on by remembering the Change of Mind trick (page 25). What pushed your blood up to your head, fighting gravity? Your heart did, acting as a little pump. Something like a pump pushed the water up, too—only this time, the pump was invisible. Can you guess what it was? Here's a clue: It's all over the place. It's the air!

# Air secret

The air is made up of a huge number of molecules that constantly bang into one another like miniature billiard balls. The temperature of the air tells us how fast the molecules are moving. The hotter the air, the faster the molecules move. The cooler the air, the slower the molecules move. A source of heat, like a flame or the sun, can give energy to slow-moving molecules and speed them up. It can turn cold air into hot air.

As you lowered the glass over the Viking ship, the air inside the glass got warmer from the burning matches. The molecules of air inside the glass then started moving very fast, and a lot of them escaped from the glass before it was completely lowered. This caused the air in the glass to become less dense.

When the glass completely covered the cork, the matches went out because they used up all the oxygen (they need a constant supply of oxygen to keep burning). Meanwhile, the water outside the glass was being pushed down by all the air molecules banging into it. The air inside the glass was pushing down, too, but there were fewer molecules in the glass than before. Remember, some escaped when it was hot. That means the density of the air inside the glass was less than the density of air outside it. So the air outside the glass pushed more than the air inside it did, forcing the water in and up the glass.

The sun heats the air in the same way to produce storms. By heating the air, the sun causes the air's density to lessen, and wind is the result. Why? Because cool high-density air rushes into an area of warm low-density air. If powerful enough, wind (especially the wind in storms) can lift water up out of the ocean.

# ★ dance of the butterflies

What makes the flame bright in candlelight? What makes a car go? Do you know? All around— in the sea and the ground, and in the air here and there—are chemicals that, when mixed, create amazing natural tricks!

In this magic trick, you'll produce a chemical reaction that will cause audience attraction!

## You Will Need

- sharp pencil
- large cork
- funnel
- thin tissue paper in a few bright colors
- pencil
- scissors
- sheet of thin cork
- glue
- 10 Alka-Seltzer™ tablets
- bowl
- spoon
- empty jam or jelly jar
- pitcher of water

## Getting Ready

**1** Take the pencil and push it completely through the middle of the cork to make a hole.

**2** Push the small end of the funnel through the hole as shown. Make sure it's a tight fit or your trick won't work.

**3** Lay a sheet of tissue paper over the butterfly at right and carefully trace its outline. Use the scissors to carefully cut out your butterfly.

**strip of cork**

**4** Repeat step 3 with different-colored tissue paper to make three or four butterflies.

**5** For each butterfly, cut a thin strip of sheet cork ⅛" wide and 1" long. These will be your butterflies' bodies.

**6** Glue the strips to the middle of the tissue butterflies as shown above. Let dry.

**7** Place 10 seltzer tablets in the bowl and crush them with the spoon until you have a fine powder.

**8** Put the jar, the cork with the funnel, the butterflies, the pitcher of water, and the bowl with the powder on your show table.

## Performing the Trick

**1** Look at the audience, smile, and say, "I recently visited a magical faraway land where everything was alive—rocks and socks, boxes and dishes, popcorn, candy, and anything handy. Everything was alive and dancing."

**2** Carefully pick up the tissue butterflies, show them to the audience, and say, "I made friends with these beautiful butterflies in the magical land. They were so sad when I told them I'd be leaving that I took them with me. But when I took them away from their magical home and friends, they stopped dancing and turned into mere paper butterflies."

**3** Put the butterflies back on the table and pick up the pitcher of water. Pour the water into the jar until it's half full. While pouring the water, say, "This is some water that I brought back from the magical place."

**4** Now pick up the bowl of powder and say, "And this is some of its magical white soil." Pour the powder into the jar. The water will begin to bubble.

**5** Quickly plug the top of the jar with the cork and the funnel.

**6** Pick up the butterflies and say, "I've brought you a taste of home, little ones, so you can dance once more."

**7** Place the butterflies into the top of the funnel. They will rise up and appear to fly around. Now say, "Their magic has returned. Look, they're dancing!"

# SCIENCE

Do you know why the butterflies suddenly "came to life"? Let's find out.

All the substances around you are made up of atoms. There are many different kinds of atoms, and they combine in many different ways to form all the neat stuff around you. The water in your jar is made up of two types of atoms: hydrogen and oxygen. The white powder is made up of different kinds of atoms, too. When you poured the powder into the water, it started a chemical reaction. This means the water and the powder exchanged some of their atoms. That resulted in a group of atoms splitting off from the powder in the form of a gas called carbon dioxide. The carbon dioxide gas then traveled through the water to the top of the jar.

gas pushes butterflies up

gas accumulates at top of jar

water

powder reacts with water

As more and more carbon dioxide gas accumulated at the top of the jar, pressure built up and a stream of carbon dioxide gas shot through the funnel. That pushed the paper butterflies up. As long as the water and powder reacted to produce the gas, the butterflies appeared to dance.

**50**

# mini movie

Have you ever wondered how a movie works? To find out, let's make a thaumatrope. The real magic in this trick takes place in one of the most mysterious places on Earth—your brain!

MAGIC

## You Will Need

- 8½" x 11" sheet of white paper (unruled)
- pen or pencil
- scissors
- 2" x 2" piece of stiff white cardboard

- glue or rubber cement
- large needle
- two 8" pieces of string (or thread)

## Getting Ready

**1** Put the paper on top of the pictures below and trace the circles, the bird, and the cage. Be sure to mark the Xs.

**2** Carefully cut out the two paper circles with scissors.

**3** Trace around one of these circles on the white cardboard and cut it out.

**4** Glue the paper circle with the bird onto the cardboard circle and let it dry.

**5** With the needle, poke a hole through one of the Xs on the cardboard circle. This will make it easy for you to line up the cardboard circle correctly with the other paper circle.

**6** Glue the second paper circle to the other side of the cardboard, making sure that the cage isn't upside down and that the X is over the needle hole.

**7** Use the needle to thread the pieces of string or thread through both sets of Xs.

**8** Tie the two ends of each piece of string together to keep them from slipping back through the holes. You've now completed your thaumatrope.

## Performing the Trick

**1** Show the thaumatrope to your audience. Invite a volunteer to come up and ask if he or she knows a way to get the bird inside the cage. Your volunteer will say that it's impossible because the bird is on one side of the thaumatrope and the cage is on the other.

**2** Now tell your audience: "This little bird used to be in the cage, but she escaped when I wasn't looking. If we could travel back in time, we could see the bird where she used to be—in the cage."

**3** Hold the strings in each hand as shown. Twirl the thaumatrope around and around until the strings are tightly wound.

**4** Then say, "Back through time we flow. Watch the little bird go!" While everyone is watching, pull on the strings quickly. As the thaumatrope unwinds, the bird will appear in the cage!

 SCIENCE

Do you know why the bird appeared to be in the cage when the thaumatrope unwound? Do you remember the grating you made in Grate Vision (page 18) and the way your brain stores, or remembers, a picture of what you see for a short time?

This is what happened in your magic trick when the thaumatrope unwound. Your audience continued to see the bird even after the image was gone. Here's the important point: By the time the cage appeared, your audience was still "seeing" the bird and was fooled into thinking the bird was in the cage. Their brains had *superimposed* the new cage image on the lingering bird image. Then, by the time they saw the real bird again, they superimposed it on the lingering cage image, and so on. Scientists call this persistence of vision.

The same thing happens at the movies (or "moving pictures"). If you look at a strip of movie film, you will see that it is actually a series of still pictures, one after the other. When each picture is flashed onto the movie screen, our brains remember it and merge it with the next picture. In this way, the series of still pictures appears to be moving.

the bird and cage images superimposed

So, in a way, you did time travel. You saw things the way they were just a moment ago—in the past!

# ★ dinosaurs didn't dance

All around you, at every moment, there is information in the air waiting to be decoded. Music and pictures from faraway lands, the voices of people from all over the world, and the secrets of the night sky all exist in the form of electromagnetic waves. These are the kinds of invisible waves detected by radios, televisions, and telescopes. Is it ever possible to escape these mysterious waves? By performing a magical feat, you can make the waves retreat!

MAGIC

## You Will Need

- paintbrush
- two shoe boxes with lids
- glue
- aluminum foil
- scissors
- black construction paper

- green fern leaf (or other fragrant plant)
- paints or markers
- battery-powered transistor radio

glue

## Getting Ready

**1** Use the brush to coat the inside of the first shoe box with glue. Then place a large sheet of aluminum foil in the shoe box, carefully pressing it into the corners and along the edges of the box. Let it dry, then cut off the excess foil around the edges.

**2** In the same way, line the lid of the first shoe box with foil.

**3** Now glue the black paper to the aluminum foil in the first box and lid. Be sure to cover the foil completely and cut off any excess black paper. Let dry.

**4** Rub the fern leaf against the black paper until the box smells like fern inside.

**5** Now take the second shoe box and lid and glue just the black paper to the inside of both.

**6** In big letters, paint or write *prehistoric* on the lid of the box with aluminum foil in it, and write *modern* on the lid of the box without aluminum foil. Add any designs you'd like to the boxes.

**7** Put the shoe boxes and the radio on your show table.

## Performing the Trick

**1** Start by choosing a volunteer from your audience. Then point to the two boxes on the table and say, "I have two shoe boxes. One is rather ordinary; the other is quite extraordinary. I took one of them back in time—to the age of the dinosaurs."

**2** Pick up the box labeled *prehistoric* and say, "While standing in a misty prehistoric jungle filled with giant insects and terrifying dinosaurs, I opened this magic box and filled it with the time and space around me. Though I returned to the present, the inside of this box is still in the past, 100 million years ago." Open the box, show the inside to your audience, then ask your volunteer, "Can you smell the ferns of that ancient jungle?"

**3** Now put down the shoe box and turn on the radio so everyone can hear music playing. Say, "The music you hear is made by humans using electronic devices such as this radio."

**4** Then show the inside of the *modern* box to your audience, put the radio inside, and close the lid. You will still hear the music. Say, "The music still reaches your ears because this box contains things from our time, including radio signals."

**5** Now take the radio out of the *modern* box and lower it into the *prehistoric* one. Before closing the lid, say, "But the inside of this box is from the age of the dinosaurs, long before humans made radio waves of music. There are no signals in this box for the radio to receive." Close the lid, and the music will stop!

SCIENCE

Do you know why the music stopped in one box and not the other? Remember the difference between the shoe boxes? The one with the aluminum foil in it stopped the music, and the other didn't. The secret is in the aluminum.

You can understand what's going on by using an analogy.

# Bobbing corks and wiggling particles

Even though radio waves are invisible, you can imagine what they're like by thinking about a cork floating in a pool. When a wave passes by the cork, what does the cork do? It bobs up and down. In this analogy, the waves in the pool represent radio waves, and the cork represents a charged particle inside a radio antenna. When radio waves hit charged particles on a radio's antenna, they cause the particles to bob up and down—to wiggle.

This is how radio waves are decoded into music. Information carried on the radio waves causes the charged particles in the antenna to wiggle in very precise patterns. Then the electronics in the radio read these wiggle patterns and cause a speaker to vibrate in the same pattern as the wiggles. In this way, the speaker produces the sounds you hear.

There are charged particles in the aluminum you used in your trick, too. These particles are free to move about, and they moved in response to the incoming radio waves in such a way as to neutralize them. Suddenly, your radio's antenna had no more information to decode. The charged particles in the antenna could no longer wiggle.

The *modern* box didn't shield the radio because charged particles in the cardboard, unlike those in the aluminum, are not free to move about and neutralize radio waves.

# falling reign

*There's something invisible here and there—*
*On Earth, it's nearly everywhere.*
*It constantly presses on all around.*
*In fact, it's the reason we hear every sound.*
*So let's use the push of the unseen air*
*To amaze our friends while they sit and stare!*

MAGIC

## You Will Need

- piece of clear plastic (the plastic must be larger than the mouth of the glass and thin enough to be cut with scissors, but not too thin, or it will deform under the weight of water)

- small drinking glass
- thin magic marker pen (blue is best)
- scissors
- blue food coloring
- pitcher of water

## Getting Ready

**1** For this trick, you'll need a plastic circle that's a little bit larger than the mouth of the glass and that has a tab on it. Do this by placing the glass upside down over the plastic, drawing around the glass to make a circle, then carefully cutting just outside the pen line. Be sure to leave a little tab as shown.

**2** To give the water some color, add a few drops of food coloring to the pitcher and stir.

**3** Put the glass and the pitcher on your show table.

**4** Place the plastic disk in your right hand as shown. Practice holding it so it can't be seen. This is called palming. (Note: If you are left-handed, reverse the hand instructions.)

## Performing the Trick

**1** Using your left hand, pour the water into the glass until it begins to overflow. Remember to palm the plastic disk in your right hand.

palm disk

**2** Look at the audience and say, "Oh, look—I've never known when to stop pouring. I've also never had enough sense to come in out of the rain. It's so inconvenient getting wet, so I invented a way to keep the wet rain away."

**3** Put down the pitcher, then reach for the glass with your left hand, looking as though you're about to pick it up. As you do this, reach over to the glass with your right hand. Keeping the plastic disk hidden, cover the mouth with your hand and secretly place the disk over the top. Make sure it covers the top evenly. It will stick to the mouth of the glass if centered properly.

**4** Pick up the glass with your left hand, placing your other hand over the disk. Turn the glass upside down quickly but gently. Keep the mouth of the glass tilted slightly away from the audience so they can't see the plastic.

**tilt glass away from audience, pinky on tab**

**5** Slowly remove your right hand. The disk will remain stuck to the glass and the water won't spill out.

**6** Hold the glass over your head and say, "I don't need an umbrella, do I!" Then secretly push on the little tab sticking out with your pinky. The plastic will come off and the water will fall on your head!

 SCIENCE

The plastic is holding the water in, but what's holding the plastic up? What's fighting gravity?

The answer is all around you. It's the air. The earth's gravity holds air molecules around it and doesn't allow them to escape into space. This air forms the earth's atmosphere. The weight of all that air pressing down on you is called air pressure. On a microscopic scale, air pressure on an object is the force caused by air molecules constantly colliding against the object. These collisions happen in every direction, even up.

The force of air molecules pounding up against the bottom of the plastic disk is greater than the weight of the water above the plastic disk. So the plastic disk doesn't fall. Though the water's weight may seem to be the stronger force, the air actually is!

# glassical music

*What's in your ear that allows you to hear?*
*Did you know it's a kind of drum?*
*The little drum vibrates*
*When air near you gyrates*
*To produce the music you hum.*
*From a singing cricket to a big drum's pound,*
*The shaking of molecules makes every sound.*
*So out in space or on the moon,*
*There'd be no music or song of loons*
*'Cause there isn't any air*
*Way out there.*

## MAGIC

## You Will Need

- two identical crystal wineglasses
- water
- pliers

- thin steel wire (a little longer than the diameter of the glass)
- eyedropper

## Getting Ready

**1** Fill both wineglasses about one-quarter full of water and place them about 10" to 12" apart on your table.

10" to 12" apart

**61**

**2** With the pliers, bend the steel wire at the ends and lay it over the mouth of one glass.

**3** Now hold the base of the second glass and dip a finger in the water to wet it slightly. Slowly and lightly rub the wet finger around the rim of the second glass. As your fingers follow the rim, the glass will begin to vibrate and make a high-pitched noise. When your finger becomes dry, wet it again and continue rubbing the glass.

**4** Once you can get a loud, clear tone, the steel wire on the first glass should start to vibrate. If it doesn't, use the eyedropper to add or take away water from the first glass until, by rubbing the rim of the second glass, you get the biggest vibrations possible.

**5** Set up the wire and the two glasses of water on your show table in the exact positions needed.

## Performing the Trick

**1** Look at the audience and say, "Long ago, one hundred knights in shining armor made a solemn vow to a powerful wizard. They promised to protect their village from a great beast that the wizard said would one day come and destroy them."

**2** Pick up the steel wire and hold it in front of you. Then say, "The wizard gave each knight a sliver of magic steel and told them that when the day came, the slivers would unite to make a great sword. This sword would kill the beast."

**3** Now say, "But the hundred knights were confused. They asked the wizard how they'd know when that day had arrived." Lay the wire over one glass and say, "The wizard replied that they'd know when their slivers began to dance upon a goblet of wine. He would summon them by making his own goblet sing. Then, no matter where in the world the knights were, their magical slivers would dance to the music of the wizard's goblet."

**4** Put your finger in the water and rub the glass without the wire. The wire will jump. Then open your eyes wide and say, "*I* was that wizard. And the time has come for the slivers to unite!"

# SCIENCE

Can you guess what's happening? Have you ever felt the floor shake when a stereo hit just the right note? Have you ever seen windows rattle as a big jet flew overhead? Would you believe it's merely the air that's shaking things around?

> **Frequency** refers to how fast something vibrates back and forth. **Natural frequency** is the frequency at which an object will vibrate if provided energy (for instance, if it is struck).

When you rubbed the first glass, you caused the atoms in the glass to vibrate back and forth. The vibrating atoms hit the air molecules surrounding the glass, causing the air to vibrate. The vibrating air molecules next to the glass then collided with air molecules farther away. Just like dominoes, one hitting the next, the vibration traveled from the first glass to the second one. The vibration also traveled to your ears. That's the tone you heard! When the vibrating air collided with the second glass, it caused the glass to vibrate, shaking the metal wire along with it. But why did the second glass shake? Because it had the same **natural frequency** as the first glass.

Most objects, like the glass, have a natural frequency. If the frequency of the vibrations from the first glass matches the natural frequency of the second glass, the second glass will vibrate. A similar thing happens when a swing is pushed at the right moment—it rises higher and higher. If the first glass vibrates at a different natural frequency than the second glass, not much will happen. By making the water level in the second glass just right, you made its natural frequency match the frequency of the vibrations created by the first glass.

# sands of time

Have you ever wondered how we humans tell what stuff is made of? Look at an ingredient label sometime. Even simple substances can contain a lot of different things, or ingredients. Some ancient Indian magic can help you to understand an idea scientists use to figure out what things are made of.

## You Will Need

- blue food coloring
- pitcher of water
- three small glasses
- red, white, and blue sand (available at craft stores)
- cheese grater (with a fine grating on it)
- paraffin wax (available at craft stores)

- bowl
- thin plastic tube, 8" to 10" long and ¾" in diameter (available at hardware stores)
- large glass mixing bowl
- dinner plate

## Getting Ready

**1** Add blue food coloring to the pitcher until the water is dark blue.

**2** Fill each of the three glasses with a different color of sand.

**3** Using the finest grating possible, grate the paraffin wax over the bowl until you have a good supply of paraffin shreds.

**4** Take a small handful of the red sand and mix it with some paraffin shreds. Roll the mixture in your hands like clay to form a cake with a particular shape that can fit loosely inside the plastic tube. Use just enough paraffin to make the sand cake solid.

**5** Repeat step 4 for both the white and the blue sand. It is important to make the cakes different shapes so you can tell which is which just by feeling them. Put the cakes into the plastic tube.

**6** Put the tube, the mixing bowl, the three glasses of sand, the pitcher of blue water, and the dinner plate on your table.

## Performing the Trick

**1** Look at the audience and say, "Once while traveling through ancient India, I came upon a strange and beautiful crystal-blue lake." Pick up the pitcher and pour the blue water into the mixing bowl until it's three-quarters full.

**2** Now say, "And standing in this strange lake was an even stranger old man with long white hair and crystal-blue eyes. He told me this lake was fed by three mighty rivers. Each river brought sand from faraway places, which mixed here to create this magic lake."

**3** Slowly pour the white sand into the bowl. While pouring the sand, say, "The first river brought sand from a place of great white mountains—the place where the old man was born."

**4** Now pour in the red sand and say, "The second great river brought sand from a wild red desert land—the place where the old man learned his magic."

**5** Finally, slowly pour in the blue sand and say, "And the third mighty river brought sand from a silent blue forest, where the old man found understanding and peace."

**6** Carefully put the plastic tube into the bowl. Once the tip is underwater, let the sand cakes slip out into the bowl.

**7** Mix the sand together with the tube. *Stir gently so as not to break the sand cakes and ruin the trick!*

**8** Now stop stirring and say, "Then the old man did an amazing thing. He reached into the lake and pulled out each color of sand separately. Like so!"

**9** Reach your hand into the mixing bowl and lift out each of the sand cake shapes you made, one by one. As you lift each sand cake out of the water, keep your fingers spaced like a rake so any mixed sand passes out of your hand into the water. Before you take your hand completely out of the water, close it around the sand cake. Then crush each one with your hand and sprinkle it onto the plate. As you sprinkle the white sand cake, say, "The old man said, 'This is the land in which I was born—the time of my childhood.'" With the red sand cake, say, "'This is the red land of my youth—the time of learning and adventure.'" With the blue sand cake, say, "Finally, the old man said, 'This is the land of memory—the time of peace and understanding—the place I go to now.'"

**10** Look at the audience and say, "The old man then smiled, bid me farewell, and sank into the quiet blue of the lake."

**11** Let audience members come up and try to separate the sand!

# SCIENCE

Scientists figure out what various things are made of by finding ways to separate their ingredients. For example, by heating salt water to 100° Celsius, you can find out what it's made of. The water boils away, but the salt remains. Heating separates the salt water into its two ingredients: salt and water. The idea of separating something into its parts was important to your trick.

In molding some of the sand into sand cakes, you gave the cakes a property that made them different from the regular sand. Namely, they were larger than the grains of sand, so they could not slip through your fingers. You also gave the sand cakes a property that made them different from each other: their shape. By giving each colored sand cake a different shape, you could tell which color cake you lifted out of the mixing bowl.

By using these differences between the sand cakes and the regular sand, you could separate the white, red, and blue sand in the mixing bowl—the old man's magical ingredients!

# x-ray vision

Do you ever wonder why scientists use so much complicated junk? It's because most of what happens in the universe—from giant explosions in space to the dancing of tiny atoms—is completely invisible to the naked eye. Your five senses show you only a small part of the world. Only by creating special instruments can we probe the invisible world. In this trick, you'll use an instrument to "see" through solid matter.

MAGIC

## You Will Need

- four small empty boxes (such as individual-size raisin boxes)
- small paintbrush
- white paint
- colored paint (any color will do)
- glue

- four small, fairly strong magnets
- small toy compass
- scissors
- black construction paper
- Scotch™ tape
- aluminum foil (the heavy kind works best)

## Getting Ready

**1** Open both ends of the raisin boxes, paint the outsides white, and let dry.

**2** Using the other color, paint the numbers 1, 2, 3, and 4 on your boxes. Let dry.

**3** Glue a magnet to the inside of each box as shown. The box with #1 on it should have a magnet glued above the #1, inside the box. The #2 box should have a magnet glued to the right of the #2. The magnet glued in box #3 should be glued below the #3. Finally, the magnet for box #4 should be glued to the left of the #4. Note: Before the glue dries, put the compass above each box and make sure the arrow tip points to each magnet. If the tail of the arrow points toward the magnet, spin the magnet around in its place until the compass tip points to the magnet. Then let the glue dry.

the compass arrow points up

the compass arrow points to the right

the compass arrow points down

the compass arrow points to the left

**4** Glue the ends of the boxes shut and let dry.

**5** Now line the boxes up side by side, with the numbers facing the same way. Scan the compass across the middle of the boxes and watch what happens. The needle points up on box #1, to the right on box #2, down on box #3, and to the left on box #4. You can tell which block you're over by the way the compass points!

**6** Cut the black construction paper to size, then make a tube that's about 6" long and wide enough so that the compass fits snugly inside. Use tape to keep the tube from unraveling.

paper tube with 6" compass inside

**7** Take a large sheet of aluminum foil and lay it over all four boxes, bending it over them to make a cover.

Paint an arrow on the foil. Remove the cover and set aside.

**8** Put the boxes and the aluminum cover on your show table. Also put the tube on your table, but make sure the audience can't see the compass that's inside.

## Performing the Trick

**1** Have a couple of volunteers come up to assist you.

**2** Turn your back to the volunteers and tell them to put the boxes right side up, side by side, in any order they like. They should not tell you what the order is. Then have them cover the boxes with the aluminum foil, with the arrow on it pointing right side up.

**3** Now say, "People are always trying to make things simpler and smaller. Calculators that used to be as big as rooms can now fit in your pocket. Consider X-ray machines, too. Right now they're big, complicated machines, but in the future, they'll look like this—an X-ray machine from the future!" Show the tube to your audience without letting anyone see inside it.

**4** Lean over the table and put the tube over the middle of the aluminum cover on the far left side and look into it (don't bring your eye all the way to the tube or you'll block all the light entering it). You will see the compass needle move. If it points up, the box underneath is #1. If it points right, it's #2, and so on. As you move over the different boxes with the tube, the needle will change position. Shout out the order of the boxes underneath to your audience.

# SCIENCE

Any guesses why you knew the positions of the letters without "seeing" them? The magnets inside the boxes produced an invisible field that went right through the foil and moved the compass needle in your "X-ray machine." But where did the strange invisible force of the magnets come from?

Well, inside the magnets are charged particles. These negatively charged particles are called electrons. An electron creates an invisible force field around itself, called an electric field. When electrons move, they create another kind of field. This one is called a magnetic field. Most materials contain many electrons. Since the electrons move around in many different directions, the magnetic fields they each create point in different directions, too. As a result, they cancel each other out. This is like two people pushing on a wagon in opposite directions—it won't go anywhere.

In magnetic materials, all the charged particles inside are spinning in exactly the same way so that all the little magnetic fields add up to produce a single large force field, sort of like when many people push on a wagon in the same direction. This is what is happening with each of the magnets in the boxes.

The compass needle is also magnetic. The spinning electrons in the needle are affected by the invisible magnetic fields of the magnets. As a result, the compass needle moves around as it passes over each magnet until it lines up with that magnet's spinning electrons.

## The world's biggest magnet

Can you guess why all compass needles point north? Would you believe it's because the earth is a giant magnet? Amazingly enough, deep beneath the earth's surface, trapped in an immense flowing river of molten rock, are charged particles circling around the earth's axis. The moving charges create an invisible magnetic field that spans the entire planet. It is this gigantic field that you "see" with a compass needle. Think of it—a toy compass is like a window to the inside of the earth!

# hole milk

**Parental Supervision Required**

*Most audience mind traps are set.*
*When they believe what they see, they get.*
*So here's a trick where they'll extol—*
*There's some milk when there's really a hole.*

## You Will Need

- tape measure
- clear drinking glass
- scissors
- two 8½" x 11" sheets of clear plastic acetate (¹⁄₃₂" thick)
- plastic epoxy (or use glue that dries clear)

- masking tape
- marker
- hammer
- nail
- water
- milk
- sheet of newspaper

## Getting Ready

**1** To perform this trick, first make a plastic tube that fits loosely inside the glass. Do this by taking two measurements with the tape measure: (1) the circumference of the glass and (2) its height (H). Subtract ¼" from the height measurement.

height less ¼"

circumference     height     ← circumference → measurement

Air Pressure

**2** Carefully cut a piece of plastic, using the two measurements for the height and width. (Example: If your glass measures 5" tall and 9" around, cut out a piece of plastic 4¾" x 9".)

**3** Now roll the plastic into a tube, overlapping the edge by ¼". Glue the plastic ends together, using the masking tape to hold them shut while the glue dries.

tape

**4** Now cut out a circular piece of plastic to use as a cover for the plastic tube. Do this by laying the tube end over another plastic sheet, drawing around it with a marker, then cutting it out.

**5** Using the hammer and nail, punch a small hole (about ¼" across) in the middle of the cover. Then neatly glue the cover to one end of the plastic tube and let it dry.

¼"

¼"

**6** Now test the plastic tube for leaks. Cover the hole with your finger and fill the tube with water. If there are leaks, use a little glue to fill them in after you have emptied out the water.

**7** Fill the glass about one-fifth full of milk. Then, with your finger over the hole, lower the plastic tube into the glass (open end down). The milk will be forced up into the space between the glass and the plastic, and the glass will appear full of milk (if it doesn't, add more milk). Slide your finger off the hole, but keep pushing down on the plastic. The milk will return to its original level.

milk's level with hole covered

milk's level with hole uncovered

**8** Make a cone out of your sheet of newspaper and tape it shut.

## Performing the Trick

**1** Tell your audience to excuse you for a moment while you get a glass of milk. Put the plastic tube into the milk glass while covering the hole to make the glass look full. Return to your audience.

**2** Say to your audience, "Have you ever wondered where all the stuff that magicians make disappear goes? Well, there are invisible holes in space that lead to another place. If I can find one of these invisible holes, and I've made this cone just right, then I'll funnel the milk through the hole to that other world out of sight."

**3** Pick up the newspaper cone with your free hand. Tilt the milk glass into the cone as if you were going to pour the milk in, but don't pour! Instead, secretly slide your finger sideways off the hole. The milk will settle to its real level, and it will look as if you've poured most of the milk into the cone.

**as you pretend to pour, slide finger off hole**

**4** Put the glass down, hold the cone with both hands, and walk toward your audience as if nervous about spilling the milk.

**5** As you walk, say, "I think I see a hole!" Run toward someone and pretend to trip, letting the cone fall on his or her head!

# SCIENCE

There are two secrets to this trick. One involves air pressure and the other has to do with human psychology.

When your finger was over the little hole and you lowered the plastic into the glass, the milk pushed on the air in the tube. But that air was trapped—by the plastic on all sides and by the milk on the bottom. So the air pushed back on the milk. The air pressure inside the tube was high enough, in fact, to push the milk up into the space between the glass and the plastic. When you took your finger off the hole, the milk met no resistance when it pushed on the air inside the tube. That's because that air now had a place to go—out of the hole. So the milk went into the tube.

Even though your glass was never full, the audience assumed it was when they saw milk around the sides. They compared it to something familiar—a full glass of milk—and they assumed this glass was the same without really knowing for certain. Most magic tricks work because an assumption is made on the part of the audience. The audience is fooled into believing something is true when it isn't. By contrast, good scientists try to avoid drawing conclusions about something before they have directly observed it.

# ★ which way is north? ★

**Parental Supervision Required**

No matter where in the world you are, in a South American jungle or an Arabian desert, one thing is always the same: the direction a compass needle points. Think of it—anywhere on Earth, all compass needles point to the North Pole. What draws them northward? The answer involves one of nature's grandest mysteries. The same invisible electromagnetic fields that steer a compass light the stars!

MAGIC

## You Will Need

- scissors
- 1' of thin electrical wire (16 gauge)
- masking tape
- large Band-Aid™
- red food coloring (optional)
- 12' of thick electrical wire (12 gauge)

- wire cutters (long-nose pliers can also cut wire)
- electrical tape
- dark long-sleeved shirt or jacket
- D-size battery
- compass

## Getting Ready

**1** Using the scissors, strip about ½" of the plastic insulation off the ends of the thin wire to expose the bare wire.

**2** Wrap the thin wire around your right index finger, forming a coil. (Note: If you are left-handed, reverse all these instructions.) Don't make the coil too tight—you want to be able to take it on and off easily.

**3** Twist the wire at the base of your finger. That will help the coil stay together. Tape the wires down at your palm.

**4** To hide the coil from your audience, wrap the large Band-Aid™ around it. To prevent any suspicion, you can squirt a tiny amount of red food coloring underneath the Band-Aid™ so it looks like you have a cut on your finger.

**5** Cut the long, thick wire in half with the wire cutters and strip ½" of plastic insulation off all four ends.

**6** Twist each bare end of the thin wire (the coiled one on your right hand) to a bare end of the thick wire, as shown. Then wrap electrical tape around the twisted connections.

**wrap electrical tape around exposed wire ends**

**twist wires together**

**7** Put on your long-sleeved shirt and feed the two long wires up your right sleeve, across your chest, and out of your left sleeve into your left hand.

**8** Tape one bare thick-wire end to the bottom of the D-size battery. Tape the other end so that the exposed wire lies across your left thumb. This way, when holding the battery in your left hand, you can easily bring your thumb to the battery and touch the wire end to the battery top at will.

**bare wire, taped to thumb, contacts top of battery**

**bare wire taped to bottom of battery**

**9** Put the compass on your show table. Remember, the coil is on your right index finger, the battery is in your left hand, and you connect the battery to the coil by pressing the wire on your left thumb against the top of the battery. Make sure the audience sees only the back of your right hand.

battery

wires under shirt

## Performing the Trick

**1** Begin by saying to your audience, "Once while sailing the Atlantic Ocean, I was captured by a band of pirates. They wanted to imprison me and force me to use my magic for their own evil purposes. How could I escape? I wondered. It was a dark night, and no land was in sight. They sailed guided only by their compass, so I used my magic to move their compass needle so we'd sail not to their dark island, but to my home."

**2** Put your right hand near the compass and move it around. Then say, "Take me home!" and bring your left thumb to the battery top. The compass needle will follow your right hand.

**3** Then say, "Return to north!" and take your left thumb off the battery top. The compass needle will again point to the north. Touch the battery again to show your control over the compass.

What's going on? Remember X-Ray Vision (page 68) and the way the magnets made the compass needle move?

In your trick, the battery, by a chemical reaction, created an excess of negative charges that wanted to fly away from each other. But the charges couldn't move until they had a path to flow through. When the wire on your thumb was connected to the battery, the excess negative charges got the needed path. They flowed through the wire in an **electrical current,** just as water flows through a pipe.

Then what happened? When the negative charges reached the coil, they flowed around and around, creating a magnetic field (just as the electrons circling the atoms in the magnets did in X-Ray Vision). It was this magnetic field that caused the compass needle to move.

**The flow of charges through a wire is called electrical current.**

When you disconnected the battery, the excess negative charges it produced again had no path to flow through. Therefore, the charges stopped flowing and the magnetic field disappeared.

# index